The Third Vocabulary List

This is a list of most of the third set of 350 words that children learn to understand and to say. ... based on research studies of the language development of English speaking children. No two children will learn exactly the same set of words but this list provides a guide to a core vocabulary that is common. Complete Checklist 1 (first 124 words) and Checklist 2 (second 340 words) before using this checklist. You will be using them together, as children may understand words on this checklist before they can say or sign all the words on the first and second checklists.

The balance of different types of words in the vocabulary being learned is important. Children need to learn a mix of nouns, verbs, adjectives and other parts of speech to enable them to express their ideas and to join words together in sentences. Extra spaces have been provided in each category to allow you to add words that your child understands or uses in that category, if they have some different words.

Why should you keep this record and try to ensure that your child has a vocabulary of some 800 words? Because most children enter school at 5 years of age with at least a 2,000 word vocabulary and children with Down syndrome will be disadvantaged by their limited vocabulary and grammar when they start school. In this set, many of words that children are expected to know for early reading and number work in the classroom are included.

How to use the DownsEd word list to assist your child to learn to talk

The checklist should be completed and retained by parents as they will have the most complete knowledge of their child's communication skills. Some parents will welcome the help of a home teacher or speech and language therapist as the checklist is also to be used to help to plan language teaching activities. The list is intended to be used as a supplement to the speech and language modules in the *Down Syndrome Issues and Information* series.[DSii-03-01, DSii-03-02] The information in these modules should be read before completing this checklist or starting a speech and language programme with your child. This checklist is part of a set of checklists covering all aspects of speech, language and communication skills. In addition to 3 vocabulary checklists there are checklists for interactive communication and play,[DSra-03-01] speech sounds,[DSra-02-01] and sentences and grammar.[DSra-04-01] This checklist should be used in conjunction with the other checklists as all aspects of communication skills should always be considered in parallel.

For parents

This record form is designed to be a practical aid to help you to help your child make progress. The first step is to complete the form to record the words that your child understands, signs or says at the present time. The record form can then be used to choose new words for **comprehension** activities and new words for **production** activities. The form can also be used to keep a record of your child's progress. If your child is attending a nursery, playgroup or preschool, please share this information with the staff, once you have completed the form and decided on the next words to target, as they will be able to incorporate the word practice into their activities as well. Your child is learning to talk during all of your everyday interactions, and the single most important effect on his/her rate of progress is the quality and quantity of everyday talk that he/she is included in. However, in addition, research suggests that targeted vocabulary teaching is also necessary.

To use the form

Step 1. Complete the form by recording your child's current language skills

Column 1   Place a tick and today's date in this column if you are confident that your child understands the word. If necessary, check by giving your child a choice of two objects or actions to select from, one of which is the target word.

Column 2   Place a tick and today's date in this column if your child understands and signs this word (tick for imitated signs as well as for spontaneous signs).

Column 3   Place a tick and today's date if your child understands and imitates the spoken word. Children usually say words in imitation (copy the word when they hear it) before they use the word spontaneously (without any prompt). Imitation is an important step forward and once a child begins to imitate, they begin to say more words. Imitation also provides important practise for accurate speech sound production.

Column 4   Place a tick and today's date if you have heard your child say this word spontaneously (without a prompt) in a correct context at least 3 times. A word does not have to be pronounced accurately to be credited in this column. All children take several years to learn to pronounce words as adults do from the time that they start to talk. Tick if your child uses a consistent approximation of the word with correct understanding.

Column 5   Place a tick and the date in this column when your child can say the word clearly and accurately enough to be understood by an unfamiliar listener (someone meeting your child for the first time). This is a simple measure of your child's speech clarity or phonological progress.

At this stage, all 5 columns need not be completed for every child. Some children will no longer be signing new words -they will say the new words they learn, though signing may still help them to understand new words. Columns 1,4 and 5 should be relevant for every child and speech activities will help the child's production to move from column 4 to 5. Columns 2 and

3 have been left because some children will use signs for much longer than others. Many of these children will be those with more severe speech-motor difficulties or dyspraxia and they should be receiving specialist help to develop their speech motor skills. A second group of children who will use more signs before moving to speech as their main mode of communication are those with significant and persistent hearing loss and they should have the support of a teacher for the deaf.

Typically, the child's understanding and use of a word will progress from Column 1 to Column 5 in steps. It may take many weeks for a child who understands a word to begin to say it. It may take many more months before the spoken word becomes clear. However, the more often you use the word and sign in everyday activities and games with your child, the faster he or she will progress with comprehension and production of the word.

Step 2. Choosing words for language activities.

It is important to work on both **comprehension** of new words and **production** of words already understood, so you will choose 2 separate lists of 5 target words each, one for comprehension and one for production. Choose words that you think your child will be interested in and that you feel you will be able to include in daily activities and games. You need to be able to model the word in use (that is, as it is being used naturally in a short sentence in an appropriate context). Choose the 5 words from different sections - for example, 3 nouns, 1 verb and 1 adjective or later grammar word. At this stage, you should be playing games to encourage sentence comprehension and production, so your choice of words will be influenced by this - see the *Sentence and Grammar Checklist* for more guidance. Many of the words in this list can only be taught as part of sentences - they only have meaning in a sentence, especially Helping verbs and Function words.

Put the lists of the comprehension and production words you are going to teach on the fridge or notice board and enlist the help of the rest of the family. This list will help everyone to remember to stress the use of the words as they occur in natural speech during the day. In addition, plan games to use the words. Find the objects or pictures of them. Make lotto games, find the items in picture books, hide the objects - more ideas for games are included in *Speech and Language Development for infants with Down syndrome*.[DSii-03-02]

Comprehension activities

Choose 5 words that you have not ticked in Column 1 for comprehension games and activities. Once you are confident that your child understands one of the new words because he or she responds correctly to a choice of the object, picture or action, on at least 3 occasions, tick the word and enter the date in column 1 and select another new word to teach.

Production activities

Choose 5 words for language use and speech production practice from the list of words that you have ticked in column 1 or 2 but not in column 4 or 5. These target words should start with a sound that your child can already make, so you also need to complete the *DownsEd Speech Sounds Checklist* [DSra-02-01] for your child. When you have heard the word used in imitation or spontaneously at least 3 times, mark the appropriate checklist column with a tick and the date and choose a new word to add to the list that you are teaching.

Step 3. Recording progress

Use the checklist to record your child's progress by entering each new achievement in the appropriate column with the date on which your child achieved the new vocabulary skill. Many words will be understood and used that you have not been targeting, once your child begins to talk.

You may find it helpful to keep a notebook handy to make notes during the day about all aspects of your child's communication skills, the things that he or she is wanting to communicate about and the way he or she is doing so - these observations may suggest new words to target, words that your child needs to replace the gestures or noises that they are using. You can also use your notebook as a handy record and transfer new words, gestures or speech sounds observed onto the checklists when convenient at the end of the day or week.

It is very important not to hold back your child's comprehension of new words because of delayed ability to say them. It is comprehension of words that increases his or her understanding of the world and supports the development of mental abilities.

Individual rates of progress

Many children with Down syndrome will take three years or more - from 3 years to 6 years or older, to learn to understand and sign or say these 350 words. Rates of progress will vary widely, but progress is what matters. If your child is learning new words and signs, even if only one or two each month, you will be recording progress and your child will be increasing his or her communication skills.

Remember to keep a record of your child's interactive communication and play skills,[DSra-03-01] sentence and grammar skills,[DSra-04-01] and speech sound skills,[DSra-02-01] and engage in activities to encourage progress in these skills as well as in vocabulary, so that development in each area of communication is moving forward.

Nouns

Animals

	Understands	Understands and signs	Says word in imitation	Uses word spontaneously	Understood by unfamiliar listener
animals	☐ _/_/_	☐ _/_/_	☐ _/_/_	☐ _/_/_	☐ _/_/_
ant	☐ _/_/_	☐ _/_/_	☐ _/_/_	☐ _/_/_	☐ _/_/_
hen	☐ _/_/_	☐ _/_/_	☐ _/_/_	☐ _/_/_	☐ _/_/_
wolf	☐ _/_/_	☐ _/_/_	☐ _/_/_	☐ _/_/_	☐ _/_/_
zebra	☐ _/_/_	☐ _/_/_	☐ _/_/_	☐ _/_/_	☐ _/_/_
_____	☐ _/_/_	☐ _/_/_	☐ _/_/_	☐ _/_/_	☐ _/_/_
_____	☐ _/_/_	☐ _/_/_	☐ _/_/_	☐ _/_/_	☐ _/_/_

Dressing

	Understands	Understands and signs	Says word in imitation	Uses word spontaneously	Understood by unfamiliar listener
belt	☐ _/_/_	☐ _/_/_	☐ _/_/_	☐ _/_/_	☐ _/_/_
clothes	☐ _/_/_	☐ _/_/_	☐ _/_/_	☐ _/_/_	☐ _/_/_
dressing gown	☐ _/_/_	☐ _/_/_	☐ _/_/_	☐ _/_/_	☐ _/_/_
pocket	☐ _/_/_	☐ _/_/_	☐ _/_/_	☐ _/_/_	☐ _/_/_
pyjama	☐ _/_/_	☐ _/_/_	☐ _/_/_	☐ _/_/_	☐ _/_/_
vest	☐ _/_/_	☐ _/_/_	☐ _/_/_	☐ _/_/_	☐ _/_/_
_____	☐ _/_/_	☐ _/_/_	☐ _/_/_	☐ _/_/_	☐ _/_/_
_____	☐ _/_/_	☐ _/_/_	☐ _/_/_	☐ _/_/_	☐ _/_/_

Everyday Items

	Understands	Understands and signs	Says word in imitation	Uses word spontaneously	Understood by unfamiliar listener
basket	☐ _/_/_	☐ _/_/_	☐ _/_/_	☐ _/_/_	☐ _/_/_
camera	☐ _/_/_	☐ _/_/_	☐ _/_/_	☐ _/_/_	☐ _/_/_
can	☐ _/_/_	☐ _/_/_	☐ _/_/_	☐ _/_/_	☐ _/_/_
computer	☐ _/_/_	☐ _/_/_	☐ _/_/_	☐ _/_/_	☐ _/_/_
flask	☐ _/_/_	☐ _/_/_	☐ _/_/_	☐ _/_/_	☐ _/_/_
hammer	☐ _/_/_	☐ _/_/_	☐ _/_/_	☐ _/_/_	☐ _/_/_
iron	☐ _/_/_	☐ _/_/_	☐ _/_/_	☐ _/_/_	☐ _/_/_
jar	☐ _/_/_	☐ _/_/_	☐ _/_/_	☐ _/_/_	☐ _/_/_
jug	☐ _/_/_	☐ _/_/_	☐ _/_/_	☐ _/_/_	☐ _/_/_
keyboard	☐ _/_/_	☐ _/_/_	☐ _/_/_	☐ _/_/_	☐ _/_/_
knife	☐ _/_/_	☐ _/_/_	☐ _/_/_	☐ _/_/_	☐ _/_/_
mop	☐ _/_/_	☐ _/_/_	☐ _/_/_	☐ _/_/_	☐ _/_/_
mouse	☐ _/_/_	☐ _/_/_	☐ _/_/_	☐ _/_/_	☐ _/_/_
mug	☐ _/_/_	☐ _/_/_	☐ _/_/_	☐ _/_/_	☐ _/_/_
nail	☐ _/_/_	☐ _/_/_	☐ _/_/_	☐ _/_/_	☐ _/_/_
napkin	☐ _/_/_	☐ _/_/_	☐ _/_/_	☐ _/_/_	☐ _/_/_
purse	☐ _/_/_	☐ _/_/_	☐ _/_/_	☐ _/_/_	☐ _/_/_
sheet	☐ _/_/_	☐ _/_/_	☐ _/_/_	☐ _/_/_	☐ _/_/_
string	☐ _/_/_	☐ _/_/_	☐ _/_/_	☐ _/_/_	☐ _/_/_

tape	☐ _/_/_	☐ _/_/_	☐ _/_/_	☐ _/_/_	☐ _/_/_
tissue	☐ _/_/_	☐ _/_/_	☐ _/_/_	☐ _/_/_	☐ _/_/_
tray	☐ _/_/_	☐ _/_/_	☐ _/_/_	☐ _/_/_	☐ _/_/_
_____		☐ _/_/_	☐ _/_/_	☐ _/_/_	☐ _/_/_	☐ _/_/_
_____		☐ _/_/_	☐ _/_/_	☐ _/_/_	☐ _/_/_	☐ _/_/_

Family and People

	Understands	Understands and signs	Says word in imitation	Uses word spontaneously	Understood by unfamiliar listener
clown	☐ _/_/_	☐ _/_/_	☐ _/_/_	☐ _/_/_	☐ _/_/_
cousin	☐ _/_/_	☐ _/_/_	☐ _/_/_	☐ _/_/_	☐ _/_/_
doctor	☐ _/_/_	☐ _/_/_	☐ _/_/_	☐ _/_/_	☐ _/_/_
family	☐ _/_/_	☐ _/_/_	☐ _/_/_	☐ _/_/_	☐ _/_/_
fireman	☐ _/_/_	☐ _/_/_	☐ _/_/_	☐ _/_/_	☐ _/_/_
friend	☐ _/_/_	☐ _/_/_	☐ _/_/_	☐ _/_/_	☐ _/_/_
name	☐ _/_/_	☐ _/_/_	☐ _/_/_	☐ _/_/_	☐ _/_/_
nurse	☐ _/_/_	☐ _/_/_	☐ _/_/_	☐ _/_/_	☐ _/_/_
people	☐ _/_/_	☐ _/_/_	☐ _/_/_	☐ _/_/_	☐ _/_/_
person	☐ _/_/_	☐ _/_/_	☐ _/_/_	☐ _/_/_	☐ _/_/_
police	☐ _/_/_	☐ _/_/_	☐ _/_/_	☐ _/_/_	☐ _/_/_
postman	☐ _/_/_	☐ _/_/_	☐ _/_/_	☐ _/_/_	☐ _/_/_
teacher	☐ _/_/_	☐ _/_/_	☐ _/_/_	☐ _/_/_	☐ _/_/_
_____	☐ _/_/_	☐ _/_/_	☐ _/_/_	☐ _/_/_	☐ _/_/_
_____	☐ _/_/_	☐ _/_/_	☐ _/_/_	☐ _/_/_	☐ _/_/_

Home

	Understands	Understands and signs	Says word in imitation	Uses word spontaneously	Understood by unfamiliar listener
bookcase	☐ _/_/_	☐ _/_/_	☐ _/_/_	☐ _/_/_	☐ _/_/_
cage	☐ _/_/_	☐ _/_/_	☐ _/_/_	☐ _/_/_	☐ _/_/_
classroom	☐ _/_/_	☐ _/_/_	☐ _/_/_	☐ _/_/_	☐ _/_/_
drawer	☐ _/_/_	☐ _/_/_	☐ _/_/_	☐ _/_/_	☐ _/_/_
dryer	☐ _/_/_	☐ _/_/_	☐ _/_/_	☐ _/_/_	☐ _/_/_
furniture	☐ _/_/_	☐ _/_/_	☐ _/_/_	☐ _/_/_	☐ _/_/_
home	☐ _/_/_	☐ _/_/_	☐ _/_/_	☐ _/_/_	☐ _/_/_
ironing board	☐ _/_/_	☐ _/_/_	☐ _/_/_	☐ _/_/_	☐ _/_/_
ladder	☐ _/_/_	☐ _/_/_	☐ _/_/_	☐ _/_/_	☐ _/_/_
piano	☐ _/_/_	☐ _/_/_	☐ _/_/_	☐ _/_/_	☐ _/_/_
shelves	☐ _/_/_	☐ _/_/_	☐ _/_/_	☐ _/_/_	☐ _/_/_
shower	☐ _/_/_	☐ _/_/_	☐ _/_/_	☐ _/_/_	☐ _/_/_
steps	☐ _/_/_	☐ _/_/_	☐ _/_/_	☐ _/_/_	☐ _/_/_
stool	☐ _/_/_	☐ _/_/_	☐ _/_/_	☐ _/_/_	☐ _/_/_
_____	☐ _/_/_	☐ _/_/_	☐ _/_/_	☐ _/_/_	☐ _/_/_
_____	☐ _/_/_	☐ _/_/_	☐ _/_/_	☐ _/_/_	☐ _/_/_

Meals and Snacks

	Understands	Understands and signs	Says word in imitation	Uses word spontaneously	Understood by unfamiliar listener
chocolate	☐ / /	☐ / /	☐ / /	☐ / /	☐ / /
coke	☐ / /	☐ / /	☐ / /	☐ / /	☐ / /
cracker	☐ / /	☐ / /	☐ / /	☐ / /	☐ / /
food	☐ / /	☐ / /	☐ / /	☐ / /	☐ / /
grapes	☐ / /	☐ / /	☐ / /	☐ / /	☐ / /
green beans	☐ / /	☐ / /	☐ / /	☐ / /	☐ / /
lollipop	☐ / /	☐ / /	☐ / /	☐ / /	☐ / /
meals	☐ / /	☐ / /	☐ / /	☐ / /	☐ / /
nuts	☐ / /	☐ / /	☐ / /	☐ / /	☐ / /
peanut butter	☐ / /	☐ / /	☐ / /	☐ / /	☐ / /
pop	☐ / /	☐ / /	☐ / /	☐ / /	☐ / /
pudding	☐ / /	☐ / /	☐ / /	☐ / /	☐ / /
sauce	☐ / /	☐ / /	☐ / /	☐ / /	☐ / /
soup	☐ / /	☐ / /	☐ / /	☐ / /	☐ / /
strawberries	☐ / /	☐ / /	☐ / /	☐ / /	☐ / /
sweetcorn	☐ / /	☐ / /	☐ / /	☐ / /	☐ / /
tuna	☐ / /	☐ / /	☐ / /	☐ / /	☐ / /
vitamins	☐ / /	☐ / /	☐ / /	☐ / /	☐ / /
_____	☐ / /	☐ / /	☐ / /	☐ / /	☐ / /
_____	☐ / /	☐ / /	☐ / /	☐ / /	☐ / /

Numbers

	Understands	Understands and signs	Says word in imitation	Uses word spontaneously	Understood by unfamiliar listener
six	☐ / /	☐ / /	☐ / /	☐ / /	☐ / /
seven	☐ / /	☐ / /	☐ / /	☐ / /	☐ / /
eight	☐ / /	☐ / /	☐ / /	☐ / /	☐ / /
nine	☐ / /	☐ / /	☐ / /	☐ / /	☐ / /
ten	☐ / /	☐ / /	☐ / /	☐ / /	☐ / /
eleven	☐ / /	☐ / /	☐ / /	☐ / /	☐ / /
twelve	☐ / /	☐ / /	☐ / /	☐ / /	☐ / /
numbers	☐ / /	☐ / /	☐ / /	☐ / /	☐ / /
_____	☐ / /	☐ / /	☐ / /	☐ / /	☐ / /
_____	☐ / /	☐ / /	☐ / /	☐ / /	☐ / /

Outside

	Understands	Understands and signs	Says word in imitation	Uses word spontaneously	Understood by unfamiliar listener
armband	☐ / /	☐ / /	☐ / /	☐ / /	☐ / /
cloud	☐ / /	☐ / /	☐ / /	☐ / /	☐ / /
crossing	☐ / /	☐ / /	☐ / /	☐ / /	☐ / /
doctor's	☐ / /	☐ / /	☐ / /	☐ / /	☐ / /
fair	☐ / /	☐ / /	☐ / /	☐ / /	☐ / /
farm	☐ / /	☐ / /	☐ / /	☐ / /	☐ / /
field	☐ / /	☐ / /	☐ / /	☐ / /	☐ / /

	Understands	Understands and signs	Says word in imitation	Uses word spontaneously	Understood by unfamiliar listener
flag	☐ / /	☐ / /	☐ / /	☐ / /	☐ / /
flats	☐ / /	☐ / /	☐ / /	☐ / /	☐ / /
hose	☐ / /	☐ / /	☐ / /	☐ / /	☐ / /
hospital	☐ / /	☐ / /	☐ / /	☐ / /	☐ / /
indoors	☐ / /	☐ / /	☐ / /	☐ / /	☐ / /
lawnmower	☐ / /	☐ / /	☐ / /	☐ / /	☐ / /
library	☐ / /	☐ / /	☐ / /	☐ / /	☐ / /
outdoors	☐ / /	☐ / /	☐ / /	☐ / /	☐ / /
pavement	☐ / /	☐ / /	☐ / /	☐ / /	☐ / /
rainbow	☐ / /	☐ / /	☐ / /	☐ / /	☐ / /
road	☐ / /	☐ / /	☐ / /	☐ / /	☐ / /
roof	☐ / /	☐ / /	☐ / /	☐ / /	☐ / /
rubber ring	☐ / /	☐ / /	☐ / /	☐ / /	☐ / /
shed	☐ / /	☐ / /	☐ / /	☐ / /	☐ / /
snowman	☐ / /	☐ / /	☐ / /	☐ / /	☐ / /
stick	☐ / /	☐ / /	☐ / /	☐ / /	☐ / /
stone	☐ / /	☐ / /	☐ / /	☐ / /	☐ / /
street	☐ / /	☐ / /	☐ / /	☐ / /	☐ / /
sunshine	☐ / /	☐ / /	☐ / /	☐ / /	☐ / /
traffic-lights	☐ / /	☐ / /	☐ / /	☐ / /	☐ / /
wheelbarrow	☐ / /	☐ / /	☐ / /	☐ / /	☐ / /
wind	☐ / /	☐ / /	☐ / /	☐ / /	☐ / /
woods	☐ / /	☐ / /	☐ / /	☐ / /	☐ / /
_____	☐ / /	☐ / /	☐ / /	☐ / /	☐ / /

Play

	Understands	Understands and signs	Says word in imitation	Uses word spontaneously	Understood by unfamiliar listener
bat	☐ / /	☐ / /	☐ / /	☐ / /	☐ / /
chalk	☐ / /	☐ / /	☐ / /	☐ / /	☐ / /
crayon	☐ / /	☐ / /	☐ / /	☐ / /	☐ / /
dominoes	☐ / /	☐ / /	☐ / /	☐ / /	☐ / /
glue	☐ / /	☐ / /	☐ / /	☐ / /	☐ / /
pencil	☐ / /	☐ / /	☐ / /	☐ / /	☐ / /
play	☐ / /	☐ / /	☐ / /	☐ / /	☐ / /
play dough	☐ / /	☐ / /	☐ / /	☐ / /	☐ / /
puzzle	☐ / /	☐ / /	☐ / /	☐ / /	☐ / /
story	☐ / /	☐ / /	☐ / /	☐ / /	☐ / /
_____	☐ / /	☐ / /	☐ / /	☐ / /	☐ / /

Social Words / Events

	Understands	Understands and signs	Says word in imitation	Uses word spontaneously	Understood by unfamiliar listener
birthday	☐ / /	☐ / /	☐ / /	☐ / /	☐ / /
christmas	☐ / /	☐ / /	☐ / /	☐ / /	☐ / /
holiday	☐ / /	☐ / /	☐ / /	☐ / /	☐ / /
shopping	☐ / /	☐ / /	☐ / /	☐ / /	☐ / /
snack	☐ / /	☐ / /	☐ / /	☐ / /	☐ / /

The Body

	Understands	Understands and signs	Says word in imitation	Uses word spontaneously	Understood by unfamiliar listener
ankle	☐ _/_/_	☐ _/_/_	☐ _/_/_	☐ _/_/_	☐ _/_/_
back	☐ _/_/_	☐ _/_/_	☐ _/_/_	☐ _/_/_	☐ _/_/_
body	☐ _/_/_	☐ _/_/_	☐ _/_/_	☐ _/_/_	☐ _/_/_
chin	☐ _/_/_	☐ _/_/_	☐ _/_/_	☐ _/_/_	☐ _/_/_
lips	☐ _/_/_	☐ _/_/_	☐ _/_/_	☐ _/_/_	☐ _/_/_
nails	☐ _/_/_	☐ _/_/_	☐ _/_/_	☐ _/_/_	☐ _/_/_
penis	☐ _/_/_	☐ _/_/_	☐ _/_/_	☐ _/_/_	☐ _/_/_
shoulder	☐ _/_/_	☐ _/_/_	☐ _/_/_	☐ _/_/_	☐ _/_/_
vagina	☐ _/_/_	☐ _/_/_	☐ _/_/_	☐ _/_/_	☐ _/_/_
_____	☐ _/_/_	☐ _/_/_	☐ _/_/_	☐ _/_/_	☐ _/_/_

Time

	Understands	Understands and signs	Says word in imitation	Uses word spontaneously	Understood by unfamiliar listener
after	☐ _/_/_	☐ _/_/_	☐ _/_/_	☐ _/_/_	☐ _/_/_
afternoon	☐ _/_/_	☐ _/_/_	☐ _/_/_	☐ _/_/_	☐ _/_/_
before	☐ _/_/_	☐ _/_/_	☐ _/_/_	☐ _/_/_	☐ _/_/_
minute	☐ _/_/_	☐ _/_/_	☐ _/_/_	☐ _/_/_	☐ _/_/_
next	☐ _/_/_	☐ _/_/_	☐ _/_/_	☐ _/_/_	☐ _/_/_
once	☐ _/_/_	☐ _/_/_	☐ _/_/_	☐ _/_/_	☐ _/_/_
time	☐ _/_/_	☐ _/_/_	☐ _/_/_	☐ _/_/_	☐ _/_/_
tomorrow	☐ _/_/_	☐ _/_/_	☐ _/_/_	☐ _/_/_	☐ _/_/_
yesterday	☐ _/_/_	☐ _/_/_	☐ _/_/_	☐ _/_/_	☐ _/_/_
_____	☐ _/_/_	☐ _/_/_	☐ _/_/_	☐ _/_/_	☐ _/_/_

Transport

	Understands	Understands and signs	Says word in imitation	Uses word spontaneously	Understood by unfamiliar listener
helicopter	☐ _/_/_	☐ _/_/_	☐ _/_/_	☐ _/_/_	☐ _/_/_
trike/tricycle	☐ _/_/_	☐ _/_/_	☐ _/_/_	☐ _/_/_	☐ _/_/_
snack	☐ _/_/_	☐ _/_/_	☐ _/_/_	☐ _/_/_	☐ _/_/_
van	☐ _/_/_	☐ _/_/_	☐ _/_/_	☐ _/_/_	☐ _/_/_
_____	☐ _/_/_	☐ _/_/_	☐ _/_/_	☐ _/_/_	☐ _/_/_

Verbs

Helping Verbs / Auxiliaries

	Understands	Understands and signs	Says word in imitation	Uses word spontaneously	Understood by unfamiliar listener
am	☐ _/_/_	☐ _/_/_	☐ _/_/_	☐ _/_/_	☐ _/_/_
are	☐ _/_/_	☐ _/_/_	☐ _/_/_	☐ _/_/_	☐ _/_/_
be	☐ _/_/_	☐ _/_/_	☐ _/_/_	☐ _/_/_	☐ _/_/_
can	☐ _/_/_	☐ _/_/_	☐ _/_/_	☐ _/_/_	☐ _/_/_
can't	☐ _/_/_	☐ _/_/_	☐ _/_/_	☐ _/_/_	☐ _/_/_

could	☐ _/_/_	☐ _/_/_	☐ _/_/_	☐ _/_/_	☐ _/_/_
did	☐ _/_/_	☐ _/_/_	☐ _/_/_	☐ _/_/_	☐ _/_/_
do	☐ _/_/_	☐ _/_/_	☐ _/_/_	☐ _/_/_	☐ _/_/_
does	☐ _/_/_	☐ _/_/_	☐ _/_/_	☐ _/_/_	☐ _/_/_
don't	☐ _/_/_	☐ _/_/_	☐ _/_/_	☐ _/_/_	☐ _/_/_
going	☐ _/_/_	☐ _/_/_	☐ _/_/_	☐ _/_/_	☐ _/_/_
has	☐ _/_/_	☐ _/_/_	☐ _/_/_	☐ _/_/_	☐ _/_/_
have	☐ _/_/_	☐ _/_/_	☐ _/_/_	☐ _/_/_	☐ _/_/_
is	☐ _/_/_	☐ _/_/_	☐ _/_/_	☐ _/_/_	☐ _/_/_
let	☐ _/_/_	☐ _/_/_	☐ _/_/_	☐ _/_/_	☐ _/_/_
may	☐ _/_/_	☐ _/_/_	☐ _/_/_	☐ _/_/_	☐ _/_/_
must	☐ _/_/_	☐ _/_/_	☐ _/_/_	☐ _/_/_	☐ _/_/_
need	☐ _/_/_	☐ _/_/_	☐ _/_/_	☐ _/_/_	☐ _/_/_
not	☐ _/_/_	☐ _/_/_	☐ _/_/_	☐ _/_/_	☐ _/_/_
should	☐ _/_/_	☐ _/_/_	☐ _/_/_	☐ _/_/_	☐ _/_/_
try	☐ _/_/_	☐ _/_/_	☐ _/_/_	☐ _/_/_	☐ _/_/_
want to	☐ _/_/_	☐ _/_/_	☐ _/_/_	☐ _/_/_	☐ _/_/_
was	☐ _/_/_	☐ _/_/_	☐ _/_/_	☐ _/_/_	☐ _/_/_
were	☐ _/_/_	☐ _/_/_	☐ _/_/_	☐ _/_/_	☐ _/_/_
will	☐ _/_/_	☐ _/_/_	☐ _/_/_	☐ _/_/_	☐ _/_/_
won't	☐ _/_/_	☐ _/_/_	☐ _/_/_	☐ _/_/_	☐ _/_/_
would	☐ _/_/_	☐ _/_/_	☐ _/_/_	☐ _/_/_	☐ _/_/_

Verbs - Actions

	Understands	Understands and signs	Says word in imitation	Uses word spontaneously	Understood by unfamiliar listener
answer	☐ _/_/_	☐ _/_/_	☐ _/_/_	☐ _/_/_	☐ _/_/_
bake	☐ _/_/_	☐ _/_/_	☐ _/_/_	☐ _/_/_	☐ _/_/_
buy	☐ _/_/_	☐ _/_/_	☐ _/_/_	☐ _/_/_	☐ _/_/_
call	☐ _/_/_	☐ _/_/_	☐ _/_/_	☐ _/_/_	☐ _/_/_
carry	☐ _/_/_	☐ _/_/_	☐ _/_/_	☐ _/_/_	☐ _/_/_
catch	☐ _/_/_	☐ _/_/_	☐ _/_/_	☐ _/_/_	☐ _/_/_
have	☐ _/_/_	☐ _/_/_	☐ _/_/_	☐ _/_/_	☐ _/_/_
change	☐ _/_/_	☐ _/_/_	☐ _/_/_	☐ _/_/_	☐ _/_/_
chew	☐ _/_/_	☐ _/_/_	☐ _/_/_	☐ _/_/_	☐ _/_/_
choose	☐ _/_/_	☐ _/_/_	☐ _/_/_	☐ _/_/_	☐ _/_/_
collect	☐ _/_/_	☐ _/_/_	☐ _/_/_	☐ _/_/_	☐ _/_/_
colour in	☐ _/_/_	☐ _/_/_	☐ _/_/_	☐ _/_/_	☐ _/_/_
copy	☐ _/_/_	☐ _/_/_	☐ _/_/_	☐ _/_/_	☐ _/_/_
count	☐ _/_/_	☐ _/_/_	☐ _/_/_	☐ _/_/_	☐ _/_/_
cover	☐ _/_/_	☐ _/_/_	☐ _/_/_	☐ _/_/_	☐ _/_/_
crawl	☐ _/_/_	☐ _/_/_	☐ _/_/_	☐ _/_/_	☐ _/_/_
cut out	☐ _/_/_	☐ _/_/_	☐ _/_/_	☐ _/_/_	☐ _/_/_
dig	☐ _/_/_	☐ _/_/_	☐ _/_/_	☐ _/_/_	☐ _/_/_
drop	☐ _/_/_	☐ _/_/_	☐ _/_/_	☐ _/_/_	☐ _/_/_
dry	☐ _/_/_	☐ _/_/_	☐ _/_/_	☐ _/_/_	☐ _/_/_
end	☐ _/_/_	☐ _/_/_	☐ _/_/_	☐ _/_/_	☐ _/_/_
feel	☐ _/_/_	☐ _/_/_	☐ _/_/_	☐ _/_/_	☐ _/_/_

fill	☐ _/_/_	☐ _/_/_	☐ _/_/_	☐ _/_/_	☐ _/_/_
fit	☐ _/_/_	☐ _/_/_	☐ _/_/_	☐ _/_/_	☐ _/_/_
fix	☐ _/_/_	☐ _/_/_	☐ _/_/_	☐ _/_/_	☐ _/_/_
float	☐ _/_/_	☐ _/_/_	☐ _/_/_	☐ _/_/_	☐ _/_/_
fly	☐ _/_/_	☐ _/_/_	☐ _/_/_	☐ _/_/_	☐ _/_/_
follow	☐ _/_/_	☐ _/_/_	☐ _/_/_	☐ _/_/_	☐ _/_/_
hate	☐ _/_/_	☐ _/_/_	☐ _/_/_	☐ _/_/_	☐ _/_/_
hear	☐ _/_/_	☐ _/_/_	☐ _/_/_	☐ _/_/_	☐ _/_/_
hold	☐ _/_/_	☐ _/_/_	☐ _/_/_	☐ _/_/_	☐ _/_/_
hop	☐ _/_/_	☐ _/_/_	☐ _/_/_	☐ _/_/_	☐ _/_/_
join	☐ _/_/_	☐ _/_/_	☐ _/_/_	☐ _/_/_	☐ _/_/_
knock	☐ _/_/_	☐ _/_/_	☐ _/_/_	☐ _/_/_	☐ _/_/_
laugh	☐ _/_/_	☐ _/_/_	☐ _/_/_	☐ _/_/_	☐ _/_/_
lick	☐ _/_/_	☐ _/_/_	☐ _/_/_	☐ _/_/_	☐ _/_/_
live	☐ _/_/_	☐ _/_/_	☐ _/_/_	☐ _/_/_	☐ _/_/_
listen	☐ _/_/_	☐ _/_/_	☐ _/_/_	☐ _/_/_	☐ _/_/_
loose	☐ _/_/_	☐ _/_/_	☐ _/_/_	☐ _/_/_	☐ _/_/_
make	☐ _/_/_	☐ _/_/_	☐ _/_/_	☐ _/_/_	☐ _/_/_
march	☐ _/_/_	☐ _/_/_	☐ _/_/_	☐ _/_/_	☐ _/_/_
match	☐ _/_/_	☐ _/_/_	☐ _/_/_	☐ _/_/_	☐ _/_/_
mix	☐ _/_/_	☐ _/_/_	☐ _/_/_	☐ _/_/_	☐ _/_/_
move	☐ _/_/_	☐ _/_/_	☐ _/_/_	☐ _/_/_	☐ _/_/_
paddle	☐ _/_/_	☐ _/_/_	☐ _/_/_	☐ _/_/_	☐ _/_/_
paint	☐ _/_/_	☐ _/_/_	☐ _/_/_	☐ _/_/_	☐ _/_/_
paste	☐ _/_/_	☐ _/_/_	☐ _/_/_	☐ _/_/_	☐ _/_/_
pick	☐ _/_/_	☐ _/_/_	☐ _/_/_	☐ _/_/_	☐ _/_/_
point	☐ _/_/_	☐ _/_/_	☐ _/_/_	☐ _/_/_	☐ _/_/_
pour	☐ _/_/_	☐ _/_/_	☐ _/_/_	☐ _/_/_	☐ _/_/_
pretend	☐ _/_/_	☐ _/_/_	☐ _/_/_	☐ _/_/_	☐ _/_/_
remember	☐ _/_/_	☐ _/_/_	☐ _/_/_	☐ _/_/_	☐ _/_/_
rip	☐ _/_/_	☐ _/_/_	☐ _/_/_	☐ _/_/_	☐ _/_/_
roll	☐ _/_/_	☐ _/_/_	☐ _/_/_	☐ _/_/_	☐ _/_/_
scratch	☐ _/_/_	☐ _/_/_	☐ _/_/_	☐ _/_/_	☐ _/_/_
shake	☐ _/_/_	☐ _/_/_	☐ _/_/_	☐ _/_/_	☐ _/_/_
shear	☐ _/_/_	☐ _/_/_	☐ _/_/_	☐ _/_/_	☐ _/_/_
skip	☐ _/_/_	☐ _/_/_	☐ _/_/_	☐ _/_/_	☐ _/_/_
slide	☐ _/_/_	☐ _/_/_	☐ _/_/_	☐ _/_/_	☐ _/_/_
smell	☐ _/_/_	☐ _/_/_	☐ _/_/_	☐ _/_/_	☐ _/_/_
start	☐ _/_/_	☐ _/_/_	☐ _/_/_	☐ _/_/_	☐ _/_/_
stick	☐ _/_/_	☐ _/_/_	☐ _/_/_	☐ _/_/_	☐ _/_/_
stir	☐ _/_/_	☐ _/_/_	☐ _/_/_	☐ _/_/_	☐ _/_/_
swallow	☐ _/_/_	☐ _/_/_	☐ _/_/_	☐ _/_/_	☐ _/_/_
sweep	☐ _/_/_	☐ _/_/_	☐ _/_/_	☐ _/_/_	☐ _/_/_
taste	☐ _/_/_	☐ _/_/_	☐ _/_/_	☐ _/_/_	☐ _/_/_
tear	☐ _/_/_	☐ _/_/_	☐ _/_/_	☐ _/_/_	☐ _/_/_
tell	☐ _/_/_	☐ _/_/_	☐ _/_/_	☐ _/_/_	☐ _/_/_
think	☐ _/_/_	☐ _/_/_	☐ _/_/_	☐ _/_/_	☐ _/_/_

turn off/on	☐ _/ /_	☐ _/ /_	☐ _/ /_	☐ _/ /_	☐ _/ /_
undress	☐ _/ /_	☐ _/ /_	☐ _/ /_	☐ _/ /_	☐ _/ /_
wake	☐ _/ /_	☐ _/ /_	☐ _/ /_	☐ _/ /_	☐ _/ /_
without	☐ _/ /_	☐ _/ /_	☐ _/ /_	☐ _/ /_	☐ _/ /_
write	☐ _/ /_	☐ _/ /_	☐ _/ /_	☐ _/ /_	☐ _/ /_

Adjectives

Adjectives - Describing Words

	Understands	Understands and signs	Says word in imitation	Uses word spontaneously	Understood by unfamiliar listener
awake	☐ _/ /_	☐ _/ /_	☐ _/ /_	☐ _/ /_	☐ _/ /_
better	☐ _/ /_	☐ _/ /_	☐ _/ /_	☐ _/ /_	☐ _/ /_
fine	☐ _/ /_	☐ _/ /_	☐ _/ /_	☐ _/ /_	☐ _/ /_
first	☐ _/ /_	☐ _/ /_	☐ _/ /_	☐ _/ /_	☐ _/ /_
high	☐ _/ /_	☐ _/ /_	☐ _/ /_	☐ _/ /_	☐ _/ /_
last	☐ _/ /_	☐ _/ /_	☐ _/ /_	☐ _/ /_	☐ _/ /_
mad	☐ _/ /_	☐ _/ /_	☐ _/ /_	☐ _/ /_	☐ _/ /_
new	☐ _/ /_	☐ _/ /_	☐ _/ /_	☐ _/ /_	☐ _/ /_
poor	☐ _/ /_	☐ _/ /_	☐ _/ /_	☐ _/ /_	☐ _/ /_
windy	☐ _/ /_	☐ _/ /_	☐ _/ /_	☐ _/ /_	☐ _/ /_

Colours

	Understands	Understands and signs	Says word in imitation	Uses word spontaneously	Understood by unfamiliar listener
black	☐ _/ /_	☐ _/ /_	☐ _/ /_	☐ _/ /_	☐ _/ /_
brown	☐ _/ /_	☐ _/ /_	☐ _/ /_	☐ _/ /_	☐ _/ /_
orange	☐ _/ /_	☐ _/ /_	☐ _/ /_	☐ _/ /_	☐ _/ /_
pink	☐ _/ /_	☐ _/ /_	☐ _/ /_	☐ _/ /_	☐ _/ /_
white	☐ _/ /_	☐ _/ /_	☐ _/ /_	☐ _/ /_	☐ _/ /_

Movement

	Understands	Understands and signs	Says word in imitation	Uses word spontaneously	Understood by unfamiliar listener
fast	☐ _/ /_	☐ _/ /_	☐ _/ /_	☐ _/ /_	☐ _/ /_
quick	☐ _/ /_	☐ _/ /_	☐ _/ /_	☐ _/ /_	☐ _/ /_
slow	☐ _/ /_	☐ _/ /_	☐ _/ /_	☐ _/ /_	☐ _/ /_

Personal Qualities

	Understands	Understands and signs	Says word in imitation	Uses word spontaneously	Understood by unfamiliar listener
angry	☐ _/ /_	☐ _/ /_	☐ _/ /_	☐ _/ /_	☐ _/ /_
disgusted	☐ _/ /_	☐ _/ /_	☐ _/ /_	☐ _/ /_	☐ _/ /_
excited	☐ _/ /_	☐ _/ /_	☐ _/ /_	☐ _/ /_	☐ _/ /_
frightened	☐ _/ /_	☐ _/ /_	☐ _/ /_	☐ _/ /_	☐ _/ /_
sad	☐ _/ /_	☐ _/ /_	☐ _/ /_	☐ _/ /_	☐ _/ /_
scared	☐ _/ /_	☐ _/ /_	☐ _/ /_	☐ _/ /_	☐ _/ /_

surprised	☐ __/__/__	☐ __/__/__	☐ __/__/__	☐ __/__/__	☐ __/__/__
worried	☐ __/__/__	☐ __/__/__	☐ __/__/__	☐ __/__/__	☐ __/__/__

Quantity

	Understands	Understands and signs	Says word in imitation	Uses word spontaneously	Understood by unfamiliar listener
any	☐ __/__/__	☐ __/__/__	☐ __/__/__	☐ __/__/__	☐ __/__/__
empty	☐ __/__/__	☐ __/__/__	☐ __/__/__	☐ __/__/__	☐ __/__/__
full	☐ __/__/__	☐ __/__/__	☐ __/__/__	☐ __/__/__	☐ __/__/__
half	☐ __/__/__	☐ __/__/__	☐ __/__/__	☐ __/__/__	☐ __/__/__
many	☐ __/__/__	☐ __/__/__	☐ __/__/__	☐ __/__/__	☐ __/__/__
much	☐ __/__/__	☐ __/__/__	☐ __/__/__	☐ __/__/__	☐ __/__/__

Size

	Understands	Understands and signs	Says word in imitation	Uses word spontaneously	Understood by unfamiliar listener
fat	☐ __/__/__	☐ __/__/__	☐ __/__/__	☐ __/__/__	☐ __/__/__
heavy	☐ __/__/__	☐ __/__/__	☐ __/__/__	☐ __/__/__	☐ __/__/__
light	☐ __/__/__	☐ __/__/__	☐ __/__/__	☐ __/__/__	☐ __/__/__
long	☐ __/__/__	☐ __/__/__	☐ __/__/__	☐ __/__/__	☐ __/__/__
tall	☐ __/__/__	☐ __/__/__	☐ __/__/__	☐ __/__/__	☐ __/__/__
thick	☐ __/__/__	☐ __/__/__	☐ __/__/__	☐ __/__/__	☐ __/__/__
thin	☐ __/__/__	☐ __/__/__	☐ __/__/__	☐ __/__/__	☐ __/__/__
tiny	☐ __/__/__	☐ __/__/__	☐ __/__/__	☐ __/__/__	☐ __/__/__
short	☐ __/__/__	☐ __/__/__	☐ __/__/__	☐ __/__/__	☐ __/__/__

Sound

	Understands	Understands and signs	Says word in imitation	Uses word spontaneously	Understood by unfamiliar listener
loud	☐ __/__/__	☐ __/__/__	☐ __/__/__	☐ __/__/__	☐ __/__/__
noisy	☐ __/__/__	☐ __/__/__	☐ __/__/__	☐ __/__/__	☐ __/__/__
quiet	☐ __/__/__	☐ __/__/__	☐ __/__/__	☐ __/__/__	☐ __/__/__

Textures

	Understands	Understands and signs	Says word in imitation	Uses word spontaneously	Understood by unfamiliar listener
furry	☐ __/__/__	☐ __/__/__	☐ __/__/__	☐ __/__/__	☐ __/__/__
sticky	☐ __/__/__	☐ __/__/__	☐ __/__/__	☐ __/__/__	☐ __/__/__

Prepositions

Place

	Understands	Understands and signs	Says word in imitation	Uses word spontaneously	Understood by unfamiliar listener
about	☐ __/__/__	☐ __/__/__	☐ __/__/__	☐ __/__/__	☐ __/__/__
above	☐ __/__/__	☐ __/__/__	☐ __/__/__	☐ __/__/__	☐ __/__/__
around	☐ __/__/__	☐ __/__/__	☐ __/__/__	☐ __/__/__	☐ __/__/__
at	☐ __/__/__	☐ __/__/__	☐ __/__/__	☐ __/__/__	☐ __/__/__

behind	☐ _/_/_	☐ _/_/_	☐ _/_/_	☐ _/_/_	☐ _/_/_
beside	☐ _/_/_	☐ _/_/_	☐ _/_/_	☐ _/_/_	☐ _/_/_
by	☐ _/_/_	☐ _/_/_	☐ _/_/_	☐ _/_/_	☐ _/_/_
first	☐ _/_/_	☐ _/_/_	☐ _/_/_	☐ _/_/_	☐ _/_/_
from	☐ _/_/_	☐ _/_/_	☐ _/_/_	☐ _/_/_	☐ _/_/_
in front	☐ _/_/_	☐ _/_/_	☐ _/_/_	☐ _/_/_	☐ _/_/_
into	☐ _/_/_	☐ _/_/_	☐ _/_/_	☐ _/_/_	☐ _/_/_
last	☐ _/_/_	☐ _/_/_	☐ _/_/_	☐ _/_/_	☐ _/_/_
next to	☐ _/_/_	☐ _/_/_	☐ _/_/_	☐ _/_/_	☐ _/_/_
of	☐ _/_/_	☐ _/_/_	☐ _/_/_	☐ _/_/_	☐ _/_/_
on top of	☐ _/_/_	☐ _/_/_	☐ _/_/_	☐ _/_/_	☐ _/_/_
over	☐ _/_/_	☐ _/_/_	☐ _/_/_	☐ _/_/_	☐ _/_/_
through	☐ _/_/_	☐ _/_/_	☐ _/_/_	☐ _/_/_	☐ _/_/_
to	☐ _/_/_	☐ _/_/_	☐ _/_/_	☐ _/_/_	☐ _/_/_
with	☐ _/_/_	☐ _/_/_	☐ _/_/_	☐ _/_/_	☐ _/_/_
_____	☐ _/_/_	☐ _/_/_	☐ _/_/_	☐ _/_/_	☐ _/_/_

Pronouns

Possessives

	Understands	Understands and signs	Says word in imitation	Uses word spontaneously	Understood by unfamiliar listener
their	☐ _/_/_	☐ _/_/_	☐ _/_/_	☐ _/_/_	☐ _/_/_
theirs	☐ _/_/_	☐ _/_/_	☐ _/_/_	☐ _/_/_	☐ _/_/_
ours	☐ _/_/_	☐ _/_/_	☐ _/_/_	☐ _/_/_	☐ _/_/_
yours	☐ _/_/_	☐ _/_/_	☐ _/_/_	☐ _/_/_	☐ _/_/_

Pronouns

	Understands	Understands and signs	Says word in imitation	Uses word spontaneously	Understood by unfamiliar listener
he	☐ _/_/_	☐ _/_/_	☐ _/_/_	☐ _/_/_	☐ _/_/_
myself	☐ _/_/_	☐ _/_/_	☐ _/_/_	☐ _/_/_	☐ _/_/_
our	☐ _/_/_	☐ _/_/_	☐ _/_/_	☐ _/_/_	☐ _/_/_
she	☐ _/_/_	☐ _/_/_	☐ _/_/_	☐ _/_/_	☐ _/_/_
them	☐ _/_/_	☐ _/_/_	☐ _/_/_	☐ _/_/_	☐ _/_/_
these	☐ _/_/_	☐ _/_/_	☐ _/_/_	☐ _/_/_	☐ _/_/_
they	☐ _/_/_	☐ _/_/_	☐ _/_/_	☐ _/_/_	☐ _/_/_
those	☐ _/_/_	☐ _/_/_	☐ _/_/_	☐ _/_/_	☐ _/_/_
us	☐ _/_/_	☐ _/_/_	☐ _/_/_	☐ _/_/_	☐ _/_/_
we	☐ _/_/_	☐ _/_/_	☐ _/_/_	☐ _/_/_	☐ _/_/_
yourself	☐ _/_/_	☐ _/_/_	☐ _/_/_	☐ _/_/_	☐ _/_/_
_____	☐ _/_/_	☐ _/_/_	☐ _/_/_	☐ _/_/_	☐ _/_/_

Other Function Words

Question Words

	Understands	Understands and signs	Says word in imitation	Uses word spontaneously	Understood by unfamiliar listener
which	☐ _/_/_	☐ _/_/_	☐ _/_/_	☐ _/_/_	☐ _/_/_
why	☐ _/_/_	☐ _/_/_	☐ _/_/_	☐ _/_/_	☐ _/_/_

Quantifiers and Articles

	Understands	Understands and signs	Says word in imitation	Uses word spontaneously	Understood by unfamiliar listener
a	☐ _/_/_	☐ _/_/_	☐ _/_/_	☐ _/_/_	☐ _/_/_
an	☐ _/_/_	☐ _/_/_	☐ _/_/_	☐ _/_/_	☐ _/_/_
a bit	☐ _/_/_	☐ _/_/_	☐ _/_/_	☐ _/_/_	☐ _/_/_
a lot	☐ _/_/_	☐ _/_/_	☐ _/_/_	☐ _/_/_	☐ _/_/_
different	☐ _/_/_	☐ _/_/_	☐ _/_/_	☐ _/_/_	☐ _/_/_
each	☐ _/_/_	☐ _/_/_	☐ _/_/_	☐ _/_/_	☐ _/_/_
every	☐ _/_/_	☐ _/_/_	☐ _/_/_	☐ _/_/_	☐ _/_/_
lots	☐ _/_/_	☐ _/_/_	☐ _/_/_	☐ _/_/_	☐ _/_/_
some	☐ _/_/_	☐ _/_/_	☐ _/_/_	☐ _/_/_	☐ _/_/_
_____	☐ _/_/_	☐ _/_/_	☐ _/_/_	☐ _/_/_	☐ _/_/_

Connecting Words

	Understands	Understands and signs	Says word in imitation	Uses word spontaneously	Understood by unfamiliar listener
also	☐ _/_/_	☐ _/_/_	☐ _/_/_	☐ _/_/_	☐ _/_/_
another	☐ _/_/_	☐ _/_/_	☐ _/_/_	☐ _/_/_	☐ _/_/_
as	☐ _/_/_	☐ _/_/_	☐ _/_/_	☐ _/_/_	☐ _/_/_
because	☐ _/_/_	☐ _/_/_	☐ _/_/_	☐ _/_/_	☐ _/_/_
but	☐ _/_/_	☐ _/_/_	☐ _/_/_	☐ _/_/_	☐ _/_/_
for	☐ _/_/_	☐ _/_/_	☐ _/_/_	☐ _/_/_	☐ _/_/_
if	☐ _/_/_	☐ _/_/_	☐ _/_/_	☐ _/_/_	☐ _/_/_
just	☐ _/_/_	☐ _/_/_	☐ _/_/_	☐ _/_/_	☐ _/_/_
or	☐ _/_/_	☐ _/_/_	☐ _/_/_	☐ _/_/_	☐ _/_/_
so	☐ _/_/_	☐ _/_/_	☐ _/_/_	☐ _/_/_	☐ _/_/_
then	☐ _/_/_	☐ _/_/_	☐ _/_/_	☐ _/_/_	☐ _/_/_
too	☐ _/_/_	☐ _/_/_	☐ _/_/_	☐ _/_/_	☐ _/_/_
_____	☐ _/_/_	☐ _/_/_	☐ _/_/_	☐ _/_/_	☐ _/_/_

DOWN SYNDROME
resources *ra*
and activities

Down Syndrome Resources and Activities is a range of teaching materials, assessment and recording resources, designed for use with children with Down syndrome and children with similar learning difficulties.

Suitable for use at home and school, by parents, teachers, and speech and language therapists, these materials have been designed and evaluated by expert researchers and practitioners.

For the latest information on the series, see the *Down Syndrome Resources and Activities* web site at http://www.downsed.org/dsra/ or contact The Down Syndrome Educational Trust.

Series Editors

Sue Buckley is a psychologist, Emeritus Professor of Developmental Disability in the Psychology Department at the University of Portsmouth, UK and Director of Research and Training at The Down Syndrome Educational Trust. Sue has been actively involved in researching the developmental and educational needs of children with Down syndrome since 1980. She is an internationally recognised authority and has published widely for parents, professionals and researchers. One of Sue's three children, Roberta, is a young adult with Down syndrome.

Gillian Bird is a psychologist and Director of Consultancy and Education at The Down Syndrome Educational Trust. Gillian has been working with children with Down syndrome, from birth to teenage years, and their families since 1983. She has developed and supported the successful inclusion of children with Down syndrome in mainstream education since 1988. Gillian has also developed early intervention programmes and been active in research, publishing and training with colleagues.

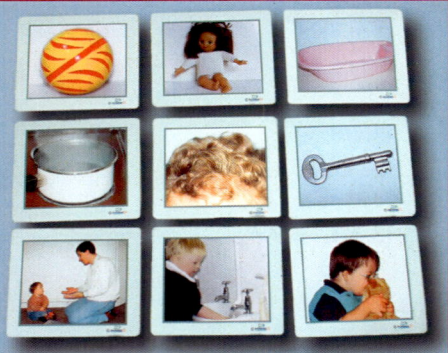

Also available from The Down Syndrome Educational Trust -

Down Syndrome Issues and Information is a unique range of publications that provide comprehensive information and practical advice about the range of developmental, health and social issues related to Down syndrome in a concise and accessible format.

DOWN SYNDROME issues and information *ii*

Written by expert researchers and practitioners, each section addresses a specific topic with a clear overview, practical guidelines and advice, and references for supporting material and additional resources.

Designed to meet the needs of parents, teachers, speech and language therapists, psychologists, and healthcare professionals, all advice and information is based on the latest scientific knowledge and wide, practical experience.

For further information, see the *Down Syndrome Issues and Information* web site at http://www.downsed.org/dsii/ or contact The Down Syndrome Educational Trust.

the DOWN SYNDROME educational trust

A registered charity, number 1062823

ISBN 978-1-903806-34-0

9 781903 806340